V- MODEL

First edition. April 2, 2025.

V-Model

To all the software engineers, developers, testers, and project managers who relentlessly strive for excellence in building reliable, high-quality systems. Your dedication to rigorous processes, meticulous planning, and unwavering commitment to quality inspire us all. May this book serve as a guide and reminder of the power of structure and thoroughness in creating software that stands the test of time.

And to those who are just beginning their journey with the V-Model — may it empower you to build with confidence, precision, and a deep sense of craftsmanship.

Introduction

The Software Development Life Cycle (SDLC) methodologies have evolved over time to improve the process of software development. Here's a brief history of how these methodologies developed:

1. Waterfall Model (1970s)

 - The Waterfall model is one of the earliest SDLC methodologies. It is a linear, sequential approach where each phase must be completed before the next begins.

 - **Phases**: Requirements gathering, design, implementation, testing, deployment, and maintenance.

 - **Strengths**: Simplicity and clarity.

 - **Challenges**: Lack of flexibility, no room for changes once the project starts, and high risk if requirements were misunderstood early on.

2. *Prototyping Model (1980s)*

- The Prototyping model focuses on building prototypes (early, simplified versions of the system) to gather feedback from users.

- The feedback is then used to refine and evolve the system through iterations.

- **Strengths**: Quick feedback and early user involvement.

- **Challenges**: May lead to scope creep, and the prototype may not always meet all user requirements.

3. *Spiral Model (1986)*

- Introduced by Barry Boehm, the Spiral model combines elements of both the Waterfall and Prototyping models.

- It focuses on iterative development with frequent risk assessment and customer feedback at each iteration.

- **Strengths**: Emphasis on risk management and adaptability.

- **Challenges**: Complex to manage and requires specialised expertise.

4. Agile Methodology (2001)

- Agile emerged as a reaction against the rigidity of Waterfall and other traditional approaches.

- Manifesto for Agile Software Development was published in 2001, emphasising collaboration, flexibility, customer feedback, and incremental development.

- Popular frameworks: Scrum, Kanban, XP (Extreme Programming).

- **Strengths**: Flexibility, faster releases, continuous feedback, and adaptability.

- **Challenges**: Requires high levels of collaboration and can be difficult to scale in large projects.

5. Scrum (1995)

- Scrum, a popular Agile framework, focuses on short development cycles called sprints.

- It emphasises team collaboration, daily stand-ups, and continuous delivery of working software.

- **Strengths**: Frequent delivery of working software, improved team communication.

- **Challenges**: Requires a significant cultural shift and skilled leadership.

6. DevOps (2010s)

- DevOps is an extension of Agile that emphasises collaboration between development and operations teams.

- Its goal is to shorten the development life cycle and deliver high-quality software continuously.

- **Strengths**: Faster delivery of updates, improved collaboration between teams.

- **Challenges**: Requires significant infrastructure and tooling, and a shift in organisational culture.

7. Lean Software Development (2000s)

- Based on Lean manufacturing principles, Lean focuses on eliminating waste, improving efficiency, and delivering value to the customer.

- **Strengths**: More efficient processes, faster delivery.

- **Challenges**: Requires a cultural shift and careful balancing of efficiency with quality.

The SDLC methodologies have evolved from rigid, linear approaches to more flexible, iterative models that allow for faster, more efficient, and higher-quality software delivery. Each methodology has its strengths and weaknesses, and the choice of methodology often depends on the project's needs, scale, and the team's experience.

Introduction to the V-Model

The V-Model (also known as the Verification and Validation model) is an extension of the traditional Waterfall Model, emphasising a clear, structured approach to software development with a focus on validation and verification at every stage of the development process.

The V-Model gets its name from the shape of the process flow, which resembles the letter "V". The left side of the "V" represents the stages of definition and design, while the right side represents validation and verification activities. The bottom of the "V" is the actual coding phase, where development occurs.

Phases of the V-Model

1. Requirements Analysis (Left side of the "V")
  - Detailed requirements for the system are gathered from the client and stakeholders. This phase ensures that the project's scope and objectives are clearly defined.

  - This is analogous to the initial phase in the Waterfall model.

2. System Design (Left side of the "V")
  - High-level design and architecture of the system are developed. This includes defining the system's structure, components, and interfaces.

  - This phase leads to the development of detailed system specifications.

V-Model

3. Architecture Design (Left side of the "V")

- The detailed architecture of the system is designed, including the design of modules, data flow, and system interaction.

4. Module Design (Left side of the "V")

- Detailed design of individual software components (modules) takes place in this phase, focusing on functionality, data flow, and interaction between components.

5. Coding (Bottom of the "V")

- The actual software coding begins based on the designs and specifications. This is the phase where developers implement the software.

6. Unit Testing (Right side of the "V")

- After coding, the system undergoes unit testing, which is aimed at validating the individual components (modules) to ensure they work as expected.

7. Integration Testing (Right side of the "V")

- Once individual components pass unit testing, they are integrated and tested as a whole. This phase checks if the system's components work together as intended.

8. System Testing (Right side of the "V")

- This phase involves testing the entire system to ensure it meets the functional and non-functional requirements. It's a validation step to verify that the system works as a whole.

9. Acceptance Testing (Right side of the "V")

- The final phase where the software is tested by the client or end users to verify it meets the original requirements and expectations.

Verification and Validation

- **Verification**: This refers to ensuring that the system is being built according to the design and specifications. This happens during the phases on the left side of the "V" (e.g., during requirements analysis, design, and coding).

- **Validation**: This involves ensuring that the system meets the business and user needs. It occurs during testing phases on the right side of the "V," such as system and acceptance testing.

Place of the V-Model in the SDLC Landscape

The V-Model holds a significant place in the SDLC landscape due to its structured and disciplined approach, which enhances the reliability of software systems. It is often considered an extension of the Waterfall model with the key difference being the parallelism between development activities and their corresponding testing activities.

1. Advantages:

- **Early Detection of Defects:** By emphasising verification and validation at every stage, the V-Model helps catch errors early in the development process.

V-Model

- **Clear and Structured**: The model offers a clear, step-by-step approach that is easy to follow, making it ideal for smaller projects with well-defined requirements.

- **No Overlapping Phases**: Each phase has clear deliverables and milestones, which can make the development process predictable.

2. Disadvantages:

- **Inflexibility**: Similar to the Waterfall model, the V-Model can be rigid. Once a phase is completed, it is difficult to go back and make changes, making it less suitable for projects with evolving requirements.

- **Late Testing**: Even though there is an emphasis on testing, it still happens after development, which may lead to challenges if defects are found late in the process.

- **Not Ideal for Complex, Large Projects**: The V-Model can be cumbersome for large projects where requirements are likely to change or evolve over time.

When to Use the V-Model

- **Stable Requirements**: The V-Model works well when the project requirements are well-understood and unlikely to change throughout the development cycle.

- **Small to Medium Projects**: The V-Model is most effective for small to medium-sized projects where the complexity is low, and development is straightforward.

- **Regulated Industries**: It is often used in industries like healthcare, aerospace, and automotive, where rigorous testing and validation are required to meet regulatory standards.

The V-Model brings a structured, disciplined approach to the software development lifecycle, focusing on both verification and validation. While it shares similarities with the Waterfall model, its emphasis on parallel testing throughout the development process offers clear advantages in terms of early defect detection. However, it is best suited for projects with well-defined requirements and where changes are minimal during the development process.

The importance of following structured development processes in software engineering.

Following structured development processes in software engineering is crucial for the successful design, development, and maintenance of high-quality software. These processes provide a framework that ensures consistency, predictability, and efficiency throughout the entire software development life cycle (SDLC). Here are the key reasons why structured development processes are important:

1. Ensures Consistency and Quality
   - Structured processes provide clear guidelines and standards for software development, ensuring that all team members follow the same approach and methodologies. This consistency helps maintain

high-quality code and prevents errors due to confusion or miscommunication.

- It also makes it easier to measure quality and progress against predefined standards, leading to more reliable and maintainable software.

2. Improves Predictability and Project Planning
- Structured development processes, such as Agile, Waterfall, or V-Model, allow for better planning, estimation, and risk management. By defining phases and milestones in advance, teams can predict the duration and effort required for each stage of the project.

- This helps in setting realistic expectations for stakeholders and avoiding scope creep, leading to more controlled project timelines and budgets.

3. Facilitates Effective Communication and Collaboration
- In complex software projects, effective communication between developers, designers, testers, and stakeholders is essential. Structured processes often include regular meetings, reviews,

and checkpoints (like daily stand-ups in Agile or phase reviews in Waterfall), which help ensure everyone stays aligned on the project goals.

 - This promotes better collaboration and understanding among team members and with clients or end-users.

4. Enhances Risk Management
 - A structured approach allows teams to identify potential risks early in the development process. By performing risk analysis during the planning phase (e.g., in the Spiral Model), teams can proactively address issues before they escalate.

 - Structured methodologies also often include regular testing phases, reducing the likelihood of discovering major defects late in the project.

5. Improves Documentation and Traceability
 - Structured processes ensure that proper documentation is maintained throughout the software development life cycle. This includes requirements specifications, design documents, test cases, and user manuals.

- Good documentation provides traceability, making it easier to understand the rationale behind design decisions and changes. It also helps future developers understand the system and supports compliance with industry regulations or standards.

6. Supports Reproducibility and Maintenance

- Structured processes allow for the creation of standardised coding practices, frameworks, and tools that improve software maintainability. With well-documented processes, future updates and bug fixes can be made more efficiently.

- As software systems grow and evolve, structured processes help teams handle changes in a controlled manner, preventing potential disruptions.

7. Promotes Continuous Improvement

- Many structured processes, such as Agile and DevOps, emphasise continuous improvement. Teams are encouraged to reflect on their practices and outcomes (e.g., through retrospectives in Agile), learn from mistakes, and implement improvements in subsequent iterations.

- This cycle of feedback and improvement helps optimise both the development process and the software product itself over time.

8. Increases Customer Satisfaction

- By following a structured process that includes regular feedback from stakeholders (e.g., customers, end-users, or business owners), teams can better meet customer expectations. Structured methodologies like Agile emphasise customer collaboration and responsiveness to changing requirements.

- This leads to delivering products that are more aligned with user needs, resulting in higher customer satisfaction.

9. Facilitates Compliance and Standards Adherence

- In certain industries (e.g., healthcare, finance, aerospace), software development is subject to regulatory standards. Structured processes help ensure that all necessary regulations are met throughout the development process.

- By adhering to formalised procedures, organisations can reduce the risk of non-compliance and legal issues.

10. Supports Scalability

- Structured processes make it easier to scale development efforts, whether that means increasing team size, handling larger projects, or expanding to new markets. By having clear processes in place, larger teams can work cohesively and more efficiently.

- Structured methodologies like Agile and DevOps also support scaling by incorporating iterative cycles and automation tools that help manage large, complex software systems.

Structured development processes in software engineering are vital for ensuring that software projects are executed efficiently, on time, and to the required quality standards. By providing clear guidance, improving communication, managing risks, and ensuring compliance, these processes help minimise errors, avoid project delays, and ensure that the final product meets the needs of users and stakeholders. Whether through Waterfall, Agile, V-Model, or other frameworks, adopting a structured approach to software development is key to the success and sustainability of any software project.

The Author

Julian Cambridge was born in London, UK.

- M.Sc. Business Computing
- B.Sc. (Hons) Computing with Business

Julian founded Golden Agile Solutions to supply IT consultancy activities to clients.

- Accredited Kanban Trainer (AKT, KMP, TKP)
- Certified Scrum Professional (CSM, CSPO, A-CSM, A-CSPO, CSP-SM)
- ICAgile Authorized Instructor (Agile Fundamentals, Agile Product Ownership, Agile Testing, Business Agility)

Table of Contents

V-Model

Overview of the V-Model

The V-Model, or Verification and Validation model, is a software development methodology that emphasises testing at each stage of the software development process. It's an extension of the traditional Waterfall model but with a key difference: for every development phase, there is a corresponding testing phase, allowing for continuous validation and verification of the software. This model gets its name from the shape of the process flow, which forms a "V" — with development activities on the left side and testing activities on the right side.

What is the V-Model?

The V-Model is a linear and sequential approach to software development that emphasises validation and verification. It ensures that each stage of development is verified and validated before moving to the next phase. The model aims to catch errors early in the process by integrating testing activities throughout the development cycle, making it a disciplined approach to both development and testing.

In the V-Model, as development progresses through phases like requirements gathering, design, and implementation, corresponding validation and verification activities occur to ensure the software meets both the specified requirements and user needs.

Key Phases of the V-Model

1. Requirements Analysis (Left side of the "V")
  - **Purpose**: In this phase, the functional and non-functional requirements of the system are gathered and defined.

  - **Outcome**: A Requirements Specification document that outlines what the system must do and how it should perform.

2. System Design (Left side of the "V")

- **Purpose**: Based on the requirements, a high-level system design is created, including architecture and modules. This phase addresses how the system will meet the requirements.

- **Outcome**: A System Design Document that details the system architecture and how each component will interact.

3. Architecture Design (Left side of the "V")

- **Purpose**: Define the overall system structure, major components, interfaces, and technology choices to meet business and non-functional requirements.

- **Outcome**: A validated high-level architecture that guides detailed design and enables early risk reduction.

4. Module Design (Left side of the "V")

- **Purpose**: Break the architecture into detailed, testable modules with clear responsibilities and interactions.

 - **Outcome**: Detailed module specifications ready for development and mapped directly to unit and integration tests.

5. *Implementation (Bottom of the "V")*
 - **Purpose**: The development phase, where the actual code for the system is written based on the design documents.

 - **Outcome**: The working system or application, which is then tested for individual component functionality.

6. *Testing Phases (Right side of the "V"):*
 These phases mirror the development phases to ensure each aspect of the system is thoroughly tested and validated:

 - **Unit Testing (Right side)**: Focuses on verifying individual components or modules.

 - Corresponds to Implementation.

 - Ensures that each module is working as expected.

V-Model

- **Integration Testing (Right side)**: Tests the interaction between integrated components.

   - Corresponds to System Design.

   - Verifies that components work together and interact correctly.

- **System Testing (Right side)**: Validates the system as a whole, ensuring it meets the original requirements.

   - Corresponds to Requirements Analysis.

   - Ensures the system satisfies all functional and non-functional requirements.

- **Acceptance Testing (Right side)**: This phase involves the final validation by the client or end users to confirm that the system meets business needs.

   - Corresponds to Requirements Analysis.

   - Ensures that the system is ready for deployment and works as intended in the real-world environment.

Overview of the Sequential Flow and How It Forms a "V" Shape

The V-Model is often depicted as a "V" to highlight its two main aspects:

- *Left Side (Development Phases):* The development starts with Requirements Analysis, then moves through System Design, Architecture Design, and Module Design before reaching the Implementation phase at the bottom of the "V". This side of the "V" outlines the process of designing and building the system.

- *Right Side (Testing Phases):* After the implementation phase, the testing activities follow. Unit Testing corresponds to the module design, Integration Testing corresponds to system design, System Testing matches with the requirements phase, and Acceptance Testing ensures that the software meets user needs. Each testing phase verifies that the software behaves as expected at each corresponding development stage.

The sequential flow ensures that testing is built into the process from the beginning, and no phase is skipped. Each phase on the left side has a corresponding validation or verification phase on the right side, which ensures that issues are identified and resolved early.

Benefits of the V-Model

1. *Clear Structure:* The V-Model provides a clear, well-defined structure where each phase has specific deliverables, making it easy to follow and manage.

2. *Early Detection of Issues:* With corresponding testing phases for every development activity, defects can be caught early in the process, which helps reduce the risk of errors later in the development cycle.

3. *High Quality:* The continuous validation and verification steps ensure that the system meets both

functional and non-functional requirements, leading to higher-quality software.

4. *Predictable Outcomes:* Because the process is linear and each phase is clearly defined, it provides a predictable and controlled approach to software development, which is useful for smaller projects with well-defined requirements.

5. *Clear Documentation:* The V-Model encourages thorough documentation of each phase (requirements, design, testing), which helps in maintaining the software and makes future updates easier.

Limitations of the V-Model

1. *Inflexibility:* One of the key drawbacks of the V-Model is its rigidity. Once a phase is completed, it's difficult to go back and make changes. This makes it

less suitable for projects where requirements may evolve or change frequently.

2. Not Ideal for Complex or Large Projects: The V-Model is often less effective for large, complex projects where the requirements are unclear or constantly changing. It doesn't easily accommodate changes once the process is underway.

3. Late Testing: Although the V-Model incorporates testing into the development process, the actual testing occurs after the implementation phase, meaning that discovering major issues could potentially lead to delays in the project timeline.

4. Lack of Iteration: The V-Model doesn't encourage iterative development. It's a strictly linear process, so if issues are found during testing, the project may require going back through earlier phases, which can be time-consuming.

5. *Resource Intensive:* The strict division between development and testing activities can lead to resource constraints, particularly in smaller teams, as separate teams or personnel may be required for each phase.

The V-Model is a highly structured, sequential approach to software development that emphasises both verification and validation. While it offers clear benefits in terms of predictability, quality assurance, and early detection of issues, its rigidity and lack of flexibility can make it less suitable for projects where requirements evolve or for larger, more complex projects. However, for projects with well-defined requirements and a clear path forward, the V-Model remains an effective methodology for ensuring that the final product meets all necessary standards.

Detailed Explanation of Each Phase

1. Requirements Analysis (Left side of the "V")

- **Purpose**: The goal of the Requirements Analysis phase is to clearly define what the software system will do, from both the business and technical perspectives.

- **How to Define Clear, Precise Requirements:**

- Engage Stakeholders: Communicate with all relevant stakeholders (business owners, users, customers) to understand their needs and expectations.

- Document Functional Requirements: Specify what the system is supposed to do, such as user interactions, data handling, and key business processes.

- Document Non-Functional Requirements: Define the performance, security, scalability, and usability aspects of the system.

V-Model

- Use Cases and User Stories: Develop detailed use cases or user stories to clarify how users will interact with the system and the expected outcomes.

- Clarify Constraints: Identify constraints like regulatory requirements, hardware specifications, and technology limitations.

- Review and Sign Off: Ensure that the requirements are reviewed and approved by both technical teams and stakeholders before proceeding to the design phase.

- **Outcome**: A Requirements Specification document that serves as the foundation for the entire development process.

2. System Design (Left side of the "V")
- **Purpose**: This phase focuses on creating the high-level design and architecture of the software system. It transforms the requirements into a blueprint for the software.

- **High-Level Architecture and Design Specifications**:

V-Model

- Define System Components: Break the system down into high-level modules and define the key components or subsystems, such as databases, interfaces, and services.

- Define Interfaces: Specify how different components will interact with each other, including data flow and API specifications.

- Identify Technology Stack: Decide on programming languages, frameworks, and technologies that will be used to implement the system.

- Design Diagrams: Create high-level design diagrams such as System Architecture Diagrams, Data Flow Diagrams, and Entity Relationship Diagrams to visualise system components and their interactions.

- Define Performance and Scalability: Consider factors like load balancing, database optimisations, and other non-functional requirements.

- **Outcome**: A System Design Document that provides a clear architecture, technical specifications, and interaction details for the development team.

3. Architecture Design (Left side of the 'V')

- Purpose:

The Architecture Design phase defines the **structural blueprint of the system**. It focuses on how the system is organised at a high level and how major components, subsystems, and external systems interact with one another. This phase translates system design decisions into a clear architectural structure that guides development and integration.

- Key Activities:

- Decompose the system into major components, services, or layers

- Define interfaces, communication protocols, and data flow between components

- Identify architectural patterns (e.g. layered architecture, client–server, microservices)

- Address non-functional requirements such as performance, scalability, security, reliability, and maintainability

- Consider deployment architecture and infrastructure constraints

- Why It Matters:

Architecture Design decisions have a significant long-term impact. Poor architectural choices can lead to integration issues, performance bottlenecks, security weaknesses, and high maintenance costs. This phase ensures the system is **technically feasible, scalable, and testable** before detailed module design and coding begin.

- Outcome:

An **Architecture Design Specification** that defines components, interfaces, interaction flows, and architectural constraints. This specification becomes the foundation for both Module Design and Integration Testing.

4. Module Design (Left side of the 'V')

- Purpose:

The Module Design phase focuses on the **detailed design of individual software components**. Each module is specified in terms of its internal logic, data structures, algorithms, and responsibilities. This phase answers the question of *how each component will be built* to fulfil the architectural design.

- Key Activities:

- Define module responsibilities and boundaries

- Design internal logic, workflows, and control structures

- Specify inputs, outputs, and data structures for each module

- Define error handling, validation rules, and edge cases

- Prepare detailed design artefacts such as class diagrams, sequence diagrams, or pseudocode

- Why It Matters:

Well-designed modules improve **code quality, testability, and maintainability**. Clear module definitions reduce complexity, enable parallel development, and make defects easier to isolate. This phase ensures developers have precise guidance before implementation begins.

- Outcome:

A **Module Design Specification** that provides detailed instructions for developers and forms the basis for **Unit Testing**, where each module is validated in isolation against its design.

5. Implementation (Bottom of the "V")

- **Purpose**: In this phase, the actual coding or implementation of the system occurs. Developers translate the design into executable code.

- Writing the Actual Code:

- Translate Design to Code: Developers write code based on the system and module designs, following coding standards and best practices.

- Use Modularisation: The system is implemented in discrete modules or components to facilitate easier testing, maintenance, and future upgrades.

- Version Control: Use version control tools (like Git) to manage the codebase and track changes.

- Documentation: Maintain proper code documentation to help future developers understand the logic and structure of the code.

- **Outcome**: A working version of the software that implements the system design. The code will be tested in later phases.

6. *Unit Testing (Right side of the "V")*

- **Purpose**: After the code is written, each individual component or unit is tested to ensure it functions correctly in isolation.

- **Testing Individual Components**:

- Test Each Module Separately: Unit tests focus on validating the smallest testable parts of the application (individual functions or methods).

- Automated Testing: Unit tests are typically automated and should be run frequently to catch errors early.

- Mock Data: Use mock objects or test data to validate the behaviour of each component independently.

- Code Coverage: Ensure a high level of test coverage to verify that all paths and logic branches are tested.

- **Outcome**: Successful unit tests confirm that each component of the system works as expected before moving on to integration.

7. Integration Testing (Right side of the "V")

- **Purpose**: Once individual modules are tested, integration testing checks if these modules work together as a whole. The aim is to identify issues when components interact.

- **Verifying the System as a Whole:**

   - Test Interactions Between Components: Ensure that the integrated components communicate properly, pass data as expected, and handle errors gracefully.

   - Test Interfaces: Focus on the interactions between different system modules or subsystems and any external systems.

   - Data Flow Testing: Verify that data is correctly passed between modules and that the system behaves as expected when modules interact.

   - Regression Testing: Ensure that new changes or additions don't break previously working functionality.

- **Outcome**: An integrated system where all components work together as expected, and any integration-related issues are resolved.

8. System Testing (Right Side of the "V")

- **Purpose**: This phase involves testing the entire system as a complete entity. The goal is to ensure that the system meets the original requirements and works as intended in an end-to-end scenario.

- **End-to-End Testing of the Complete System:**

- Functional Testing: Verify that the system behaves as intended, fulfilling all the functional requirements defined during the Requirements Analysis phase.

- Non-Functional Testing: Test the system's performance, security, scalability, and usability, ensuring it meets non-functional requirements.

- System Integration Testing: Ensure that the system works in its intended environment and interacts with other systems, hardware, or external services properly.

- Error Handling: Test the system's ability to handle edge cases, failures, and user errors.

- **Outcome**: A validated and complete system that meets the business and user requirements, with all components working together as expected.

9. Acceptance Testing (Right Side of the "V")

- **Purpose**: The final phase involves testing the software with the client or end-users to ensure it meets their expectations and is ready for deployment.

- **Ensuring the Software Meets User Needs:**

- User Acceptance Testing (UAT): The client or end users test the software in a real-world scenario to validate that it meets their needs and works as expected in the production environment.

- Feedback and Refinement: Users may provide feedback for refinements or adjustments. If necessary, updates or minor fixes are made based on this feedback.

- Sign-off: Once the system meets all the user requirements, the client formally accepts the software, and the system is deemed ready for deployment.

- **Outcome**: The software is approved by the client for release and deployment into the production environment.

Connecting the Development and Testing Phases in the V-Model

The V-Model is distinct in its structure because it emphasises the close relationship between development and testing phases. The "V" shape symbolises this relationship, with development on the left side and testing on the right side, and each development phase directly correlating to a corresponding testing phase. This structure ensures that verification and validation happen continuously, making the entire process more efficient and helping catch issues early.

The "V" Shape: How Each Development Phase Has a Corresponding Testing Phase

1. Requirements Analysis (Left side of the V) ↔ Acceptance Testing (Right side of the V)

- **Development Phase:** The Requirements Analysis phase involves gathering and defining the functional and non-functional requirements of the system.

- **Testing Phase:** The corresponding Acceptance Testing phase ensures that the software meets the business needs and user expectations.

- **Connection**: Testing ensures that the system meets the original requirements, validating that the system performs what it was intended to do, from a user perspective. Acceptance testing often involves end-users to confirm that the system is ready for deployment.

2. System Design (Left side of the V) ↔ System Testing (Right side of the V)

- **Development Phase**: In System Design, the overall architecture and system components are outlined. It focuses on how the system will fulfil the requirements defined earlier.

- **Testing Phase:** System Testing is done to validate the system as a whole, making sure that all components work together correctly and meet the original specifications.

- **Connection**: System testing ensures that the design choices made in the system design phase result in a functioning system that fulfils the requirements. The focus here is on the system as a whole.

3. Architecture Design (Left side of the V) ↔ Integration Testing (Right side of the V)

- **Development Phase:** Architecture Design focuses on how the system's various components and modules will interact with each other, laying out the integration of these components.

- **Testing Phase:** Integration Testing ensures that different components, modules, and subsystems communicate with each other effectively and work as a coherent unit.

- **Connection**: Integration testing is necessary to confirm that the system's architecture and interactions between components are correctly implemented and function as intended.

4. Module Design (Left side of the V) ↔ Unit Testing (Right side of the V)

- **Development Phase:** In the Module Design phase, the system is broken down into smaller, manageable modules, detailing their individual design and functionalities.

- **Testing Phase:** Unit Testing verifies that each module or component functions correctly in isolation.

- **Connection**: Unit testing ensures that the specific design for each module is correctly implemented and behaves as expected before moving on to integration with other parts of the system.

5. Implementation (Bottom of the V) ↔ Unit Testing and Integration Testing (Right side of the V)

- **Development Phase:** Implementation involves writing the actual code for each module, based on the earlier designs.

- **Testing Phase:** Unit Testing is performed on individual components, while Integration Testing is conducted to ensure proper interactions between components.

- **Connection**: During implementation, developers write code that must be verified and validated. Unit tests ensure that each unit of code is functional on its own, while integration testing ensures that when these units are combined, they work seamlessly together.

The Importance of Early Testing in the Development Lifecycle

Early testing is one of the core principles of the V-Model. By incorporating testing at each stage of development, the model ensures that issues are detected and addressed as early as possible, which leads to multiple benefits:

1. *Early Detection of Defects:* Early testing ensures that issues are identified and corrected in the initial stages of development rather than later when they might be more costly and time-consuming to fix. For example, detecting a requirement misunderstanding or design flaw early in the process is far more efficient than finding it after implementation.

2. *Reduced Costs:* The earlier a defect is found, the less expensive it is to fix. By validating and verifying components at each stage (from requirements to design to code), the cost of fixing issues is reduced. The later a defect is detected, the more rework is required, often affecting multiple phases of the project.

3. *Increased Confidence in System Behaviour:* With each stage of development being paired with its corresponding test phase, teams can be more confident that the system will meet requirements,

function as expected, and be ready for production without significant issues. The continuous validation improves the quality and reliability of the product.

4. Facilitates Continuous Feedback: Early testing provides continuous feedback to developers, ensuring they stay aligned with user expectations and business goals. If issues arise at any stage, they can be addressed immediately, keeping the development process on track.

How Testing Is Integrated with Design and Implementation

Testing is integrated into design and implementation in the V-Model in several key ways:

1. Design-Driven Testing:
  - At each design phase (e.g., system design, architecture design, module design), the corresponding test plan is created based on the design documents. This ensures that tests are

focused on verifying whether the design specifications will lead to a working product.

- For example, in the Module Design phase, test cases for unit testing are created based on the module design. Similarly, integration test cases are prepared during the System Design phase to validate how the modules will interact.

2. Parallel Development and Testing:

- Development and testing occur in parallel, rather than waiting until all the code is written. This integration ensures that by the time the code for a particular module is written, there are predefined tests ready for execution.

- In Implementation, as the code for each module is written, it undergoes unit testing right away to ensure functionality. After that, integration testing can begin immediately after modules are combined.

3. Continuous Feedback Loops:

- Testing provides continuous feedback to development teams. If a defect is found in a unit, it is fixed before the development team moves forward, ensuring that the system is always on track. The feedback also guides design improvements if needed.

- For example, if unit testing reveals that a component doesn't function as designed, the issue is resolved before the system is further integrated or tested, reducing the impact of fixing defects later.

4. Test-Driven Development (TDD):
- The V-Model encourages practices similar to Test-Driven Development (TDD), where developers write tests before coding. This ensures that testing is integrated from the beginning, focusing on making each module work as intended before proceeding to the next phase.

- The TDD approach ensures that every piece of code has associated tests, making it more reliable and easier to maintain.

The V-Model is unique in how it connects development and testing through a structured, parallel flow of activities. Each development phase has a corresponding testing phase, forming a "V" shape that promotes early validation and verification throughout the process. By catching defects early, providing continuous feedback, and integrating testing into every phase of design and implementation, the V-Model helps ensure that the final product meets user needs, performs as expected, and is of high quality. While its rigid structure may not be suitable for all projects, its focus on early and continuous testing makes it an effective methodology for well-defined, smaller projects with clear requirements.

The Pros and Cons of the V-Model

The V-Model is a structured and methodical software development approach, but like any methodology, it has both advantages and disadvantages. Below is a breakdown of the key pros and cons of the V-Model to help understand its suitability for different types of projects.

Advantages of the V-Model

1. Clear and Structured Process:
  - The V-Model provides a clear and well-defined development process, making it easy to understand and follow for developers, testers, and stakeholders. Each phase of development corresponds directly to a testing phase, creating a straightforward workflow with clear deliverables at each step.

  - The "V" shape provides a simple visual representation of how development and testing phases are interconnected, offering transparency for all parties involved.

2. Emphasis on Testing:
  - One of the most significant advantages of the V-Model is its strong focus on testing at every stage. Testing is planned upfront and occurs alongside the development process, ensuring that issues are identified early. Each phase of development has a corresponding validation phase, which leads to fewer defects in the final product.

V-Model

- Early testing improves the overall quality of the system and reduces the risk of undetected issues that may emerge later.

3. Predictable Outcomes:

- The linear and sequential nature of the V-Model leads to predictable outcomes, especially when project requirements are clear and stable. The method allows project managers to estimate the timeline, resources, and milestones with more accuracy because of the well-defined stages.

- This predictability is especially useful for small-to-medium-sized projects with well-understood requirements and minimal scope changes.

4. Easy to Understand and Manage:

- Since the V-Model is a relatively simple and linear approach, it is easy to communicate to teams and stakeholders. It is especially effective for small projects where the requirements are unlikely to change drastically.

- The clearly defined stages of the V-Model allow for effective management and tracking of progress, making it easy to monitor the status of each phase.

5. Documentation and Traceability:

- The V-Model encourages extensive documentation at each stage, including requirement specifications, design documents, and test plans. This documentation helps maintain a clear record of project details, making it easier to track progress, address problems, and support future maintenance.

- Traceability between development and testing phases is inherent in the model, ensuring that each requirement is validated and verified at the appropriate stage.

Disadvantages of the V-Model

1. Rigidity and Inflexibility:

- Rigidity is one of the biggest drawbacks of the V-Model. Once a phase is completed, it is difficult to go back and make changes. The V-Model follows a strict, sequential flow where each phase must be completed before the next phase begins.

- This makes it challenging to accommodate changes in requirements, design, or implementation once a phase is complete, which can be problematic

in projects where the scope or requirements may
evolve over time.

2. Difficulty in Handling Changing Requirements:

- The V-Model is not well-suited for projects with
evolving or unclear requirements. Since testing only
occurs after development stages are complete, any
changes in requirements could lead to significant
delays and rework.

- It is more suited to projects where the
requirements are clearly defined from the beginning
and are unlikely to change during development.

3. Late Testing:

- Even though testing starts early, the actual system
testing and acceptance testing only occur after the
development and implementation phases are
complete. This means that large or complex issues in
the final system may not be identified until later in the
process, potentially delaying the release or requiring
costly revisions.

V-Model

- While unit and integration testing happen earlier, system-wide issues and integration problems are only detected toward the end.

4. Limited to Small to Medium-Scale Projects:

- The V-Model works best for small to medium-scale projects with well-defined, stable requirements. For larger, more complex projects that require flexibility or involve continuous changes, the V-Model may not be the most effective approach.

- Its lack of iterative processes makes it less suitable for large-scale, agile, or innovative projects where flexibility and adaptability are key to success.

5. Not Ideal for Complex or Innovative Systems:

- For projects that involve complex or innovative systems where uncertainties are common (e.g., new technologies or highly dynamic markets), the V-Model may struggle. It assumes that the system's design and functionality are relatively well understood from the beginning, which isn't always the case for cutting-edge or experimental software.

6. Potential for Overemphasis on Documentation:

- The V-Model requires extensive documentation at every phase, which can be resource-intensive. In some cases, this documentation might lead to bureaucracy, where more time is spent writing documentation than actually building or testing the software.

- This can be particularly burdensome for smaller teams or projects with rapid timelines.

7. Limited User Involvement in Early Phases:

- The V-Model assumes that the users will be involved mainly during requirement gathering and acceptance testing. It doesn't have a strong emphasis on user feedback during the iterative development or testing phases, which can lead to a product that doesn't fully align with user needs until the final testing phase.

Summary: Pros and Cons of the V-Model

Pros:
- Clear, structured approach with defined phases.

V-Model

- Strong focus on early testing and early detection of issues.

- Predictable outcomes and well-suited for projects with stable requirements.

- Easy to understand and manage, especially for small-to-medium projects.

- Promotes documentation and traceability throughout the lifecycle.

Cons:

- Rigidity in handling changes after a phase is completed.

- Difficulty in accommodating changes in requirements.

- Late system testing, which could delay the identification of significant issues.

- More suitable for small or medium projects with clear, stable requirements.

- Not ideal for complex or innovative projects requiring flexibility.

V-Model

- Potential for excessive documentation leading to inefficiencies.

- Limited user involvement during the development process until the final testing phase.

The V-Model offers a disciplined and structured approach that works well for projects where the requirements are well understood from the beginning and are unlikely to change. It ensures high-quality software by integrating testing with development, providing early validation at each stage. However, its rigidity and lack of flexibility make it less suitable for projects where requirements might evolve or when innovation and adaptability are needed.
Understanding the pros and cons of the V-Model helps in deciding whether it is the right methodology for a specific project.

Comparing the V-Model with other SDLC Models

The V-Model is one of several software development lifecycle (SDLC) models. While it shares similarities with other models like Waterfall, Agile, and Spiral, it also has its own unique features. Let's compare the V-Model to other SDLC models, highlighting key differences and the scenarios in which the V-Model is the best choice.

1. V-Model vs. Waterfall Model

Waterfall Model:

- The Waterfall model is one of the earliest SDLC models. It is a linear, sequential approach to software development where each phase must be completed before the next phase begins. It includes stages such as requirement analysis, design, implementation, testing, deployment, and maintenance.

V-Model vs. Waterfall:

- Both the V-Model and Waterfall model are linear, sequential approaches, meaning both follow a strict path from one phase to the next.

- The key difference is that the V-Model incorporates testing into every phase of development, while in the Waterfall model, testing typically begins only after the implementation phase is complete. In the V-Model, each development phase has a corresponding validation phase (e.g., unit testing for implementation, system testing for design).

Best Use Case for the V-Model over Waterfall:

- If early testing and verification are crucial, the V-Model is a better choice because testing is integrated into each phase of development, leading to early bug detection and fewer defects in the final product.

2. V-Model vs. Agile Model

Agile Model:

- The Agile model is an iterative and incremental approach to software development. It focuses on delivering small, working pieces of software quickly and continuously improving the product based on user feedback. Agile allows for frequent changes and iterative cycles (known as sprints), with regular collaboration between developers and clients.

V-Model vs. Agile:

- The V-Model is predictive and linear, meaning it is best suited for projects where the requirements are well-understood upfront and unlikely to change, while Agile is adaptive and flexible, allowing for changes in requirements as development progresses.

- The V-Model does not support changes once a phase is completed, while Agile encourages continuous feedback and adaptation to new requirements or changes throughout the project.

- In Agile, testing happens throughout each iteration, whereas in the V-Model, testing is more structured and occurs after each specific development phase.

Best Use Case for the V-Model over Agile:
- The V-Model is ideal when the project has well-defined requirements that are unlikely to change and when thorough, structured testing at each stage is crucial. For example, in regulated industries such as healthcare or aerospace, where compliance and documentation are key.

3. V-Model vs. Spiral Model

Spiral Model:
- The Spiral model is a risk-driven SDLC approach that combines elements of iterative development with the systematic aspects of the Waterfall model. It involves repeating cycles (spirals) of planning, design, implementation, and testing, each of which refines the system based on user feedback and risk assessment.

V-Model

V-Model vs. Spiral:

- The Spiral model allows for more flexibility and risk management through iterations, while the V-Model follows a more rigid, linear path.

- The V-Model is best suited when the requirements are clear and stable, and it emphasises early and thorough testing. In contrast, the Spiral model is suited for projects with uncertain requirements, allowing for frequent adjustments and incremental improvements.

Best Use Case for the V-Model over Spiral:

- The V-Model is preferred in projects where the scope and requirements are stable, and the need for early and thorough testing is critical. It is not as adaptable as the Spiral model for projects with evolving requirements.

4. V-Model vs. Incremental Model

Incremental Model:

- In the Incremental model, the system is developed and delivered in small, incremental portions or modules. Each module is built and tested independently, and new features are added as the development progresses. This model focuses on delivering usable portions of the product earlier than the final version.

V-Model vs. Incremental:

- The V-Model follows a strict sequence of phases, where testing corresponds to each development phase, while the Incremental model allows parts of the system to be developed and tested simultaneously in parallel. The Incremental model may have faster feedback from testing, as smaller, functional parts of the system are tested early.

Best Use Case for the V-Model over Incremental:

- The V-Model is better suited for projects where the requirements are clear, fixed, and must be validated at each phase. It is ideal for smaller projects with straightforward requirements, whereas the Incremental model is better when the project involves continuously evolving features.

5. V-Model vs. DevOps Model

DevOps Model:
- DevOps is a collaborative approach that blends software development and IT operations, emphasising continuous integration, continuous testing, and continuous delivery. It encourages close collaboration between developers and IT operations teams and focuses on automating repetitive tasks, such as testing, deployment, and monitoring.

V-Model vs. DevOps:
- DevOps is focused on rapid, continuous delivery of software, with feedback and testing happening at each stage of the development pipeline. The V-Model, in contrast, is more structured and sequential, with testing happening after each specific development phase.

V-Model

Best Use Case for the V-Model over DevOps:

- The V-Model is more appropriate when the software requirements and design are stable, and the need for structured, up-front validation is critical. In contrast, DevOps works best for projects that require continuous delivery, iterative updates, and constant feedback.

When is the V-Model the Best Choice?

The V-Model is most effective when:

- Requirements are well-defined and stable: The V-Model is suitable for projects with clear, detailed, and unchanging requirements. If the project scope is clearly understood from the start, the V-Model can effectively manage the development and testing phases.

- High quality and reliability are critical: Because testing is integrated at each stage of development, the V-Model is ideal for projects where early detection of defects and high-quality output are a priority.

- Regulatory compliance is required: Industries such as aerospace, healthcare, and banking, which require strict compliance with regulations, benefit from the V-Model's clear documentation and verification processes.

- Predictable outcomes are needed: Projects that require predictable timelines and clear deliverables benefit from the V-Model's structured approach.

Case Studies and Examples of V-Model Usage in Real Projects

1. Aerospace and Defence:
  - In aerospace, where safety and compliance are paramount, the V-Model is commonly used. For instance, when developing avionics software, the V-Model allows for thorough testing and validation of requirements at each phase, ensuring that all safety and regulatory standards are met.

2. Medical Software:
  - The V-Model is often employed in the development of medical devices and healthcare software, where

regulatory compliance (e.g., FDA approvals) requires clear documentation and thorough verification at each development phase. The V-Model helps ensure that software meets all functional and safety requirements before release.

3. Automotive Industry:

- In the automotive industry, particularly for systems involved in critical functions (e.g., autonomous driving systems, braking systems), the V-Model is used to ensure high reliability and safety. Extensive testing is required for each stage, making the V-Model well-suited for such projects.

4. Banking and Financial Services:

- Software used in banking often requires robust testing and compliance with strict regulations. The V-Model ensures that every requirement is tested, documented, and verified before release, making it ideal for financial applications that require precision, security, and regulatory compliance.

V-Model

While the V-Model shares some similarities with other SDLC models, it stands out because of its structured, sequential approach that integrates testing at every stage. The V-Model is best suited for projects with clear requirements, stable scope, and where high quality and reliability are essential. It is particularly beneficial for industries like aerospace, healthcare, and automotive, where compliance, safety, and thorough validation are critical. However, for projects with dynamic requirements or the need for rapid iterations, other models like Agile or Spiral may be more suitable. Understanding the strengths and limitations of each model allows teams to choose the most appropriate SDLC for their specific project needs.

Practical Applications and Case Studies of the V-Model

The V-Model has proven to be highly effective in industries where reliability, compliance, and validation are critical. By mapping each development phase to its corresponding testing phase, it ensures that the software is tested thoroughly at every step. Below are some real-world examples of projects that have successfully used the V-Model, along with tips for successful implementation and lessons learned from real projects.

1. Aerospace Industry: Development of Avionics Systems

Case Study: Avionics Software for Commercial Aircraft

V-Model

Project Description:

- In the aerospace industry, the development of avionics systems (software that controls navigation, flight, and communication) is a critical process that demands rigorous testing and validation. Avionics software needs to meet international standards like DO-178C, which requires both high reliability and compliance with strict regulations.

Application of the V-Model:

- The V-Model was applied to ensure that every phase of the avionics software development — from requirement analysis through to system testing — was meticulously validated and tested. For example:

  - During requirements analysis, clear and precise functional and non-functional requirements (e.g., performance, safety) were defined.

  - The design phase followed, where system architecture was mapped out.

  - Corresponding testing phases were planned, such as unit testing for individual software components and integration testing for verifying system interoperability.

V-Model

Lessons Learned:

- Complexity in Requirements: Defining clear, detailed requirements from the outset was critical to avoid scope creep and ensure regulatory compliance. However, it was challenging to address edge cases in complex systems, requiring constant refinement.

- Documentation Overload: Given the nature of the industry, comprehensive documentation was necessary, which at times led to challenges in balancing speed with thorough documentation.

Challenges Faced:

- Rigidity: The V-Model's sequential nature made it difficult to accommodate changes during the development cycle, especially in the later stages. Any modification required significant adjustments to the entire lifecycle, which was costly and time-consuming.

- High Costs: Due to rigorous testing and validation, the process was more time-consuming and resource-intensive compared to iterative models like Agile.

2. Healthcare Industry: Development of Medical Device Software

Case Study: Pacemaker Software Development

Project Description:
- In the healthcare industry, especially in the development of software for medical devices like pacemakers, the V-Model is ideal for ensuring safety, reliability, and regulatory compliance (e.g., FDA regulations). The software controlling such life-critical devices requires the utmost precision and cannot afford to fail.

Application of the V-Model:
- The V-Model was utilised for developing the software that monitors and controls the pacemaker. The development process was broken down into stages:

  - Requirement Analysis: Clear definitions of system behaviour, performance, and safety criteria (e.g., heart rate monitoring and electrical pulses).

V-Model

- Design: High-level system architecture and detailed component specifications.

- Testing: Rigorous unit testing for individual modules, integration testing for combining software with hardware, and system testing to ensure overall device functionality under real-world conditions.

Lessons Learned:

- Early Involvement of Regulators: Continuous interaction with regulatory bodies helped ensure compliance and minimised last-minute modifications.

- Thorough Verification: Ensuring all requirements were verified in advance, particularly in terms of safety, led to fewer post-release issues.

Challenges Faced:

- Iterative Changes: Although the requirements were clear, the need for constant verification and addressing unforeseen issues during hardware-software integration caused delays and adjustments.

- Risk of Overengineering: Given the critical nature of the software, there was a tendency to overly engineer certain components, leading to increased complexity and cost.

3. Automotive Industry: Development of Advanced Driver Assistance Systems (ADAS)

Case Study: ADAS for Autonomous Vehicles

Project Description:
- The automotive industry has seen the development of Advanced Driver Assistance Systems (ADAS), such as autonomous driving or lane departure warning systems, where ensuring both safety and performance is essential. The V-Model is well-suited for this due to its emphasis on testing and validation at every stage of development.

Application of the V-Model:
- The ADAS development followed the V-Model's strict, structured approach, with specific testing for:

  - Sensors: Unit testing of sensor data processing (e.g., camera, radar, lidar).

V-Model

- System Integration: Testing how data flows through the system for decision-making.

- End-to-End System Testing: Validating the system's ability to handle driving scenarios in real-time, including edge cases like poor weather conditions.

Lessons Learned:

- Testing in Real-World Scenarios: While simulation tools were used, real-world testing on vehicles showed that the system could behave unpredictably in certain weather conditions. This was caught during the integration testing phase.

- Modularity: The system's modular design allowed for focused testing and validation, especially for individual subsystems, which made managing complexity easier.

Challenges Faced:

- High Costs and Time Delays: The extensive testing at each phase significantly extended the development timeline. The V-Model's rigid structure did not allow for fast, iterative cycles.

- Difficulty Adapting to New Technologies: The rapid advancements in autonomous driving technologies meant that the model sometimes faced challenges in incorporating new research findings or features once the development process had begun.

4. Banking and Financial Services: Core Banking System Development

Case Study: Core Banking System for a Financial Institution

Project Description:
- In banking and finance, the V-Model was used in developing a core banking system for processing transactions, managing customer accounts, and handling financial operations. These systems must be secure, reliable, and compliant with financial regulations (e.g., SOX, PCI DSS).

V-Model

Application of the V-Model:

- The project used the V-Model to ensure all aspects of the core banking system were thoroughly tested:

  - Unit Testing: Verification of individual modules like transaction processing, account management, and security.

  - Integration Testing: Ensuring that different systems, such as databases, payment gateways, and user interfaces, worked together.

  - System Testing: Simulating high transaction loads and ensuring that the system could handle peak traffic with zero downtime.

Lessons Learned:

- Data Security: Early involvement of security experts helped address potential vulnerabilities before they became a problem during the system testing phase.

- Clear Requirements: Having well-defined requirements ensured that testing was aligned with both user expectations and regulatory standards, avoiding rework.

Challenges Faced:

- Complexity of Compliance: Ensuring that the system adhered to all relevant financial regulations was challenging and required thorough documentation and multiple validation stages.

- Longer Development Cycle: The V-Model's rigorous testing meant that the project took longer to complete, especially as updates to financial regulations and industry standards occurred.

5. Government and Defence: Secure Communication Systems

Case Study: Military Communication Systems

Project Description:

- In the government and defence sector, developing secure communication systems for military use requires ensuring that data is transmitted securely, with no risk of interception or compromise. The V-Model's emphasis on structured testing and security validation made it an ideal choice.

V-Model

Application of the V-Model:

- The communication system was built following the V-Model, with clear phases for:

  - Requirement Analysis: Gathering security and functional requirements, such as encryption standards and real-time data transmission.

  - Design: Creating secure communication protocols and architectures.

  - Testing: Extensive security testing, including penetration tests, vulnerability assessments, and encryption validation.

Lessons Learned:

- Risk Management: Early identification of security risks in the design phase allowed for the implementation of robust mitigation strategies.

- Real-Time Testing: The system's ability to handle communication in high-pressure environments was thoroughly tested in real-world military settings.

Challenges Faced:

- Handling Unknown Threats: Given the dynamic nature of cybersecurity, new vulnerabilities were discovered during integration testing, leading to additional rounds of system redesign.

- Time and Resource Intensive: Security testing, particularly penetration testing, was resource-intensive, requiring significant investment in tools, time, and expertise.

Tips for Successful Implementation of the V-Model

1. Establish Clear Requirements:

  - Begin with well-defined, unambiguous requirements to ensure smooth progress through each phase. In industries like aerospace and healthcare, these requirements are critical and must be fully understood by all stakeholders.

2. Plan for Rigorous Testing:

  - Plan for extensive testing at each stage, ensuring that each component is validated against its corresponding design phase. Use automated testing · tools where possible to speed up testing and increase accuracy.

3. Document Everything:

  - Given the structured nature of the V-Model, ensure detailed documentation of all requirements, design decisions, test cases, and test results. This is particularly important in regulated industries.

4. Involve Stakeholders Early:

  - Engage with key stakeholders, including end users, compliance officers, and security experts, during the requirements and testing phases to ensure that the product meets all user needs and regulatory requirements.

5. Prepare for Rigidity:

  - The V-Model's rigid structure can make it difficult to accommodate changes. It's essential to prepare for change control processes to handle any modifications or adjustments to requirements during the lifecycle.

The V-Model remains an excellent choice for projects in industries that require high reliability, safety, and compliance. Through real-world examples, we've seen how the V-Model's structured approach to development and testing is ideal for complex, safety-critical systems like avionics, medical devices, automotive safety systems, core banking, and government communications. While the V-Model's strengths are clear, it does come with challenges such as rigidity, high costs, and the difficulty of accommodating changes. Nevertheless, by adhering to best practices like clear requirements, early stakeholder involvement, rigorous testing, and comprehensive documentation, teams can successfully implement the V-Model and ensure high-quality software in critical industries.

Best Practices for Using the V-Model in Modern Software Development

The V-Model is a proven methodology in software development, particularly in fields where reliability, safety, and regulatory compliance are paramount. Although it is often perceived as rigid and suited for traditional waterfall-style projects, it can be effectively adapted to modern software development tools, techniques, and frameworks. By integrating the V-Model with contemporary technologies like automated testing, Continuous Integration/Continuous Deployment (CI/CD) pipelines, and modern agile frameworks, development teams can maintain its benefits while achieving greater efficiency and flexibility.

Here are best practices for applying the V-Model in today's software development landscape:

1. Adapting the V-Model to Modern Tools and Technologies

Integration with Modern Development Tools

- The traditional V-Model emphasises sequential development and testing. To stay relevant in modern development, integrate contemporary software development tools that enhance automation, collaboration, and testing at every stage. For example:

  - Version Control Systems (VCS) such as Git allow teams to efficiently manage code changes throughout the development lifecycle, even if changes are made later in the process.

  - Project Management Tools like JIRA or Trello can help define clear requirements, track progress, and assign tasks at each stage of the V-Model.

  - Modelling Tools (e.g., UML or SysML) can be used for system and software design during the design phase, enabling a clear understanding of system components and their interactions.

Collaboration with Cloud-based Tools

- Modern cloud-based tools, such as Google Cloud Platform, AWS, and Microsoft Azure, provide infrastructure that can be integrated into the V-Model to facilitate scalability and flexibility during both development and testing phases.

 - Cloud platforms can support the rapid provisioning of environments for unit testing, integration testing, and system testing. This can reduce the overhead traditionally required for setting up infrastructure in the V-Model.

2. Integrating the V-Model with Automated Testing

Automated Unit Testing

- Unit testing in the V-Model corresponds to the first development phase, and automated unit tests are essential for ensuring that individual components are validated. Tools like JUnit, TestNG, or pytest can help automate the execution of unit tests, providing faster feedback and reducing manual effort.

V-Model

- Test-driven development (TDD), an agile practice, can be integrated with the V-Model by writing automated tests before code development. This ensures that every module is tested thoroughly as it's developed.

- Code coverage tools like JaCoCo or Coveralls can be used to ensure that the unit tests cover all necessary code paths and edge cases.

Integration Testing with Automation
- As the system design is implemented and integrated, automated integration testing becomes crucial. Tools like Selenium, Postman, or RestAssured allow for the automation of integration tests, ensuring that modules interact properly.

- Automating integration tests using tools that simulate real-world usage (e.g., API requests, database queries) ensures that integration testing is done efficiently and thoroughly.

System Testing and End-to-End Automation
- During system testing, automation frameworks such as Cypress or Selenium can be used for end-to-end

testing to validate that the complete system works as expected.

  - Continuous testing through automated frameworks ensures the product's behaviour aligns with design expectations in terms of performance, security, and functional requirements.

  - For instance, automated security testing using tools like OWASP SAP can be integrated into the system testing phase to ensure that vulnerabilities are identified early.

3. Leveraging CI/CD Pipelines in the V-Model

Continuous Integration (CI)
- The V-Model can be enhanced with Continuous Integration (CI) practices, where developers frequently commit code to a shared repository. A CI server (e.g., Jenkins, Travis CI, GitLab CI) automatically runs build and unit tests to ensure that new code doesn't break the system.

  - With CI integrated into the V-Model, early unit testing becomes automatic, providing feedback on individual modules or components during the development phase.

 - Automating the build process helps ensure that code merges and changes do not disrupt the development flow, improving the speed and accuracy of development.

Continuous Deployment (CD)

- Once the system passes all phases of the V-Model's development lifecycle (design, implementation, and testing), it can be deployed automatically through Continuous Deployment (CD) pipelines.

 - Deployment automation tools like Kubernetes, Docker, or Terraform can be used to ensure that the final product is deployed in a reliable, repeatable way.

 - Continuous delivery ensures that after passing system and acceptance testing, the software can be automatically released to production, reducing the time between development and end-user delivery.

Automated Deployment and Regression Testing

- Automating the deployment pipeline ensures that when the system is moved to production, it undergoes the necessary regression testing to ensure it works across all environments.

- This is particularly important in systems where the environment configuration differs significantly from development to production.

4. Aligning the V-Model with Agile Principles

While the V-Model is inherently sequential and rigid, it can still be aligned with agile principles such as iterative development and continuous feedback.

Agile-Style Iterations Within the V-Model
- Instead of following a pure waterfall approach, consider breaking down the development process into sprints or iterations where each iteration goes through the entire V-Model cycle. This approach helps accommodate changes and iterations while still ensuring the comprehensive testing that the V-Model provides.

- For example, at the start of each sprint, developers define small sets of requirements and proceed through the V-Model phases: design, development, unit testing, integration testing, and system testing, focusing on specific features or modules.

Feedback Loops

- Agile's emphasis on frequent feedback can be integrated by using frequent user testing and acceptance testing at the end of each iteration. This ensures that user feedback is received early and adjustments are made before the software moves into the later stages of development.

5. Ensuring Traceability and Transparency in the V-Model

In modern development, particularly in regulated industries (e.g., healthcare, finance, aerospace), maintaining traceability between requirements, development, and testing is vital.

Requirements Traceability

- Tools like DOORS Next, Jama Connect, and Atlassian Jira can maintain traceability between requirements and each corresponding development and testing phase.

 - As requirements evolve (e.g., due to regulatory changes), the V-Model can ensure that each phase remains aligned with the original or updated requirements, and that changes are reflected in both the design and testing phases.

Automated Reporting

- Modern tools can generate real-time reports that track progress, such as test coverage reports, build status, and defect logs. This transparency ensures that stakeholders have up-to-date information about the status of development and testing phases.

6. Risk Management and Quality Assurance

Risk management is integral to the V-Model, especially in high-stakes projects. By utilising modern tools and frameworks, risk management can be made more effective:

- Automated Testing: Helps identify defects early, reducing the risk of critical failures in production.

- Static Code Analysis: Tools like SonarQube or Checkmarx can be integrated into the V-Model's early development phases to catch security vulnerabilities and code quality issues before they escalate.

- Risk-based Testing: Tools such as qTest can help prioritise testing efforts based on potential risks, ensuring critical functionalities are tested first.

Modernising the V-Model for Contemporary Software Development

The V-Model, traditionally seen as a sequential, rigid methodology, can be adapted to modern software development practices by leveraging automated testing, CI/CD pipelines, and contemporary frameworks. By integrating these tools into each phase of the V-Model, teams can achieve faster feedback, improved quality, and greater flexibility while still benefiting from the structured and comprehensive testing that the V-Model provides.

Key strategies for modernising the V-Model include:

- Embracing automated testing at all stages (unit, integration, system).

- Integrating with CI/CD pipelines for continuous integration and deployment.

- Using agile practices to introduce iterative development within the V-Model framework.

- Ensuring traceability and risk management using modern tools.

- Enabling real-time feedback and transparency through automated reporting and test management systems.

By adapting the V-Model to today's technologies and practices, organisations can improve efficiency, reduce time to market, and deliver high-quality software solutions.

Summary

The V-Model is a software development methodology that provides a clear, structured approach to development and testing. It is particularly suited for projects where reliability, safety, and regulatory compliance are paramount, such as in industries like aerospace, healthcare, automotive, and finance.

Recap of Key Points:

1. Structured Approach:

- The V-Model is highly structured, with clearly defined phases for requirements analysis, design, implementation, testing, and deployment. Each development phase is matched with a corresponding testing phase, which ensures rigorous validation and verification at every step.

2. Phases of the V-Model:

- **Requirements Analysis**: Gathering clear and precise user and system requirements.

- **System Design**: High-level and detailed design to map out the system's architecture.

- **Implementation**: Actual coding and construction of the system based on the design.

- **Unit Testing**: Testing individual modules or components.

- **Integration Testing**: Ensuring the system's components work together.

- **System Testing**: End-to-end testing to ensure the entire system behaves as expected.

- **Acceptance Testing**: Validating that the system meets user needs and requirements.

3. Advantages:

- **Predictability**: The V-Model provides a predictable, linear approach to software development.

- **Clear Milestones**: Each phase is clearly defined, making it easy to track progress and ensure each stage is completed before moving to the next.

- **Thorough Testing**: The model's emphasis on testing at every stage helps catch defects early, ensuring higher-quality products.

4. Disadvantages:

- **Rigidity**: The V-Model can be inflexible, making it difficult to accommodate changes once the process is underway.

- **Resource-Intensive**: The comprehensive testing and documentation can lead to higher costs and longer development times.

- **Limited Adaptability**: It's not always well-suited for fast-paced, rapidly changing environments, where flexibility is essential.

5. Modern Adaptations:

- **Automation**: The integration of automated testing, CI/CD pipelines, and modern tools can enhance the V-Model's effectiveness, making it more agile and efficient.

- **Integration with Agile**: While the V-Model is traditionally sequential, it can be adapted to work in iterative cycles, allowing for more flexibility while retaining its thorough approach to testing and validation.

 - **Traceability**: Advanced tools for requirements traceability, automated testing, and continuous feedback help teams maintain clarity and transparency throughout the development lifecycle.

The Future of the V-Model and How It Might Evolve

While the V-Model has served the software industry well for decades, it is clear that evolving technologies and modern development practices are shaping the future of software development methodologies. Here are some ways the V-Model might evolve in the future:

1. Integration with Agile and DevOps:
 - As the demand for faster delivery cycles grows, the V-Model may be integrated with agile and DevOps practices to allow for faster development while maintaining the model's rigorous testing processes. Instead of traditional waterfall-style development,

iterative development can be incorporated into the V-Model, allowing for more frequent feedback and better responsiveness to changes.

- The use of CI/CD pipelines and automated testing within the V-Model can reduce the cycle time and improve the feedback loop, making it more compatible with modern agile methodologies.

2. Increased Use of Automation:
- The future of the V-Model will likely involve further integration with AI-driven testing tools and machine learning models that can help predict defects and optimise the testing process. Automation will continue to play a major role in reducing manual intervention, ensuring faster, more reliable testing.

- Automated reporting and real-time dashboards will provide more immediate feedback to teams, helping to identify issues quickly and ensure quality at each phase of the process.

3. Flexibility with Hybrid Models:
- In response to the need for more flexibility, the V-Model might evolve into a more hybrid approach,

where elements of the V-Model are combined with other models like the Spiral model or Iterative development. This hybrid approach would allow teams to retain the rigor of the V-Model while accommodating changes and iterative testing.

4. Emphasis on Continuous Quality Assurance:

- In the future, the V-Model may shift towards a model of continuous quality assurance (QA). Rather than having distinct "testing phases," testing could be continuous throughout the lifecycle of the project, ensuring that quality is not only verified at the end but throughout the entire development process. This would help reduce bottlenecks and improve the overall flow of development.

5. Incorporation of Emerging Technologies:

- The V-Model will likely evolve to integrate with emerging technologies, such as blockchain, cloud computing, and Internet of Things (IoT). These technologies introduce new complexities that require more adaptive methodologies, and the V-Model will need to evolve to address these complexities while maintaining its focus on testing and validation.

V-Model

The V-Model continues to be a valuable methodology for projects that require high levels of reliability, safety, and compliance. Its structured approach ensures that testing and validation are deeply embedded in the development process, leading to robust and reliable software systems. While the V-Model's rigid structure may limit its flexibility, modern practices such as automated testing, CI/CD integration, and agile principles are helping to address these challenges.

The future of the V-Model will likely involve greater flexibility, automation, and integration with agile and DevOps workflows, making it more adaptable to today's fast-paced development environments. Its ability to evolve and integrate with contemporary tools and techniques will ensure its continued relevance in the software development world.

V-Model

Foundations of Scrum Agile
Education

£2.99

App Store

Google Play

V-Model

Agile Development with DevOps

Agile Project Management: Navigating Pros and Cons of Scrum, Kanban and combining them

Agile Tales

Air Traffic Control & Baggage Handling: A Kanban Story

Boundary Value Analysis

Communication Troubles of a Scrum Team

Disney's FastPass: A Queue Story

Henry Ford Assembly Line

Imperative of Software Testing: The Post Office Horizon Scandal

Introducing the Douglass Model for Agile Coaches

Kaizen: The Philosophy of Continuous Improvement for Business and Education

Mastering Software Quality Assurance: A Comprehensive Guide

McDonald's: A Kanban Story

Nightclub Entry Token System: A Kanban Story

Pizza Delivery: A Kanban Story

Scrum: Unveiling the Agile Method

Testing SaaS: A Comprehensive Guide to Software Testing for Cloud-Based Applications

V-Model